Cornerstones of Freedom

The Franklin Delano Roosevelt Memorial

ANNE PHILLIPS

CHILDREN'S PRESS®
A Division of Grolier Publishing
New York • London • Hong Kong • Sydney
Danbury, Connecticut

Visit Children's Press on the Internet at:
http://publishing.grolier.com

Library of Congress Cataloging-in-Publication Data

Phillips, Anne.
The Franklin Delano Roosevelt Memorial / Anne Phillips.
    p. cm — (Cornerstones of freedom)
  Includes index.
  Summary: Describes the construction of one of the newest Washington
monuments, a memorial to the thirty-second president.
  ISBN 0-516-21598-1 (lib. bdg.) 0-516-27165-2 (pbk.)
  1. Franklin Delano Roosevelt Memorial (Washington, D.C.)—History—
Juvenile literature. 2. Washington (D.C.)—Buildings, structures, etc.—
Juvenile literature. [1. Franklin Delano Roosevelt Memorial (Washington,
D.C.) 2. National monuments.] I. Title. II. Series.
F203.4.F73 C65 2000
975.3—dc21
                                          99-052352

GROLIER
PUBLISHING

On a small hill at the center of the National Mall in Washington, D.C., stands the Washington Monument. It honors the first president of the United States—George Washington. From this monument, people can walk to some of America's most beloved and enduring landmarks: the Lincoln Memorial, the Thomas Jefferson Memorial, the Korean War Veterans Memorial, and the Vietnam Veterans Memorial. Each year, millions of people walk up the steps leading to Abraham Lincoln's chair or run their hands over the name of a loved one lost in Vietnam. These memorials comfort Americans and reflect their shared history.

Nearby, a short walk from the Mall in West Potomac Park, is the newest national memorial—the Franklin Delano Roosevelt Memorial. It is located along a long row of Japanese flowering cherry trees and between the Tidal Basin and the Potomac River. The memorial honors the thirty-second U.S. president, the only person elected to that office four times. By placing a memorial of him near those of other esteemed leaders—Washington, Jefferson, and Lincoln—Congress showed its utmost respect for Franklin Delano Roosevelt (FDR).

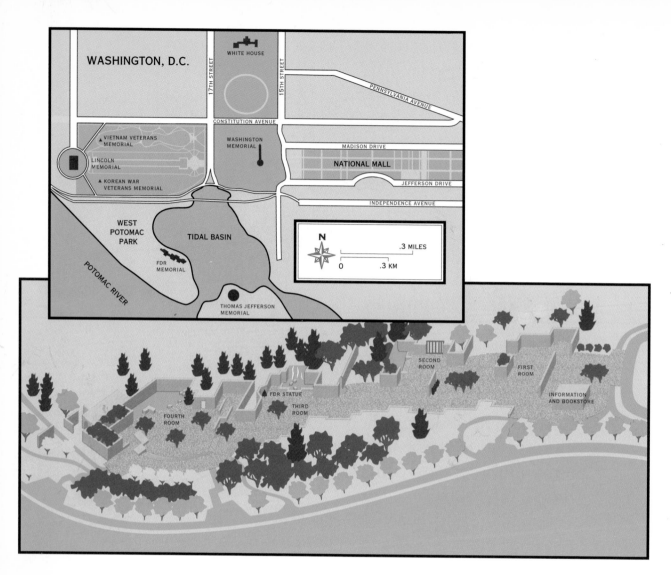

The FDR Memorial is near the National Mall (top) in Washington, D.C. The FDR Memorial (bottom) has four rooms—one for each of President Roosevelt's terms in office.

Born on January 30, 1882, Roosevelt grew up as the only child of a wealthy family. He lived in a mansion on the banks of the Hudson River in Hyde Park, New York. After graduating from Harvard University in 1903, he entered Columbia Law School in 1904. One year later, he married a distant cousin, Anna Eleanor Roosevelt. Her uncle and Franklin's cousin, Theodore Roosevelt, was the president of the

Franklin and Eleanor Roosevelt. They were married on St. Patrick's Day—March 17, 1905.

Theodore Roosevelt

United States from 1901 to 1909. Theodore's accomplishment proved an inspiration for Franklin, who had begun to show an interest in politics.

In 1911, Franklin ran for—and narrowly won—a seat in the New York State Senate. He held this position for two terms. His success in that large state drew the attention of national politicians. In 1913, President Woodrow Wilson appointed him assistant secretary of the U.S. Navy Department (a position his cousin Theodore had once held). In 1920, the Democratic Party picked Franklin as its vice presidential candidate. He and James Cox, the presidential candidate, lost that election, marking the first major setback in Roosevelt's life.

Discouraged, Roosevelt retreated with his family. In 1921, while on vacation at one of the family's homes on Campobello Island, off New Brunswick, Canada, he was stricken with polio. The disease permanently damaged his muscles. The young, athletic man was paralyzed from the waist down, unable to walk or even stand without metal braces and assistance from others. Roosevelt was devastated. He suffered severe pain for months, but as he regained his strength, he began looking for some way to improve his condition. He opened a camp for polio victims in Warm Springs, Georgia. At the camp, patients could do special exercises in the fresh spring water. He strengthened his upper body, but Roosevelt's legs did not heal.

FDR (center, right) in the pool at Warm Springs, Georgia, in 1930

For a long time, he doubted if he could ever return to public life because he could not stand to shake a voter's hand. Eleanor knew her husband would suffer more if he allowed his disability to deprive him not only of his legs but also of his political career. He took his wife's advice and ran for office. In 1929, he became the governor of New York.

That same year, when Herbert Hoover was president, many people and businesses in the United States began to have financial problems. When the stock market crashed on October 29, 1929, many people were instantly penniless, and many banks closed. Workers across the United States lost their jobs. Though there were many problems in the U.S. economy before the stock-market crash, most historians agree that the crash started the Great Depression of the 1930s. It was the worst economic slump in U.S. history.

An unemployed man sells apples in New York City during the Depression.

Roosevelt had learned from living with polio that it is best to maintain a positive outlook during a difficult time. He thought he could solve the nation's problems. In 1932, he decided to run for president against Hoover. Roosevelt promised Americans a New Deal, a program that would create new government agencies and provide jobs for workers. Desperate for change, Americans overwhelmingly voted him into office in 1932.

During the twelve years that Roosevelt served as president, Americans struggled through the Great Depression (1929– 1930s) and World War II (1941–1945). Roosevelt never spoke in public of his battle with polio. Privately, he used the lessons he had learned from his own struggle to guide him. He understood

Herbert Hoover (left) greets FDR (right). They rode together to FDR's first inauguration in 1933.

pain, loss, and fear. Under his leadership, the United States eventually triumphed. When he died of a brain hemorrhage in Warm Springs, Georgia, on April 12, 1945, the nation—and the world—mourned him. Many people wept as though they had known him personally and considered him a member of their family.

A year after his death, Congress began the process of authorizing the Franklin Delano Roosevelt Commission. It would plan a memorial to the late president. In 1955, the commission was established. It held contests to choose an architect for the project. One of the guidelines was that the design would display "the character and work of Franklin Delano Roosevelt to give us the theme of a memorial that will do him the honor he deserves and transmit his image to future generations." Although the site for the memorial was reserved in September 1959, it was another fifteen years before the commission approved the final design for the memorial. Two designs had been approved in the 1960s, but they were rejected later, causing delays in the project.

In the meantime, on April 12, 1965, a small memorial was dedicated to mark the twentieth anniversary of Roosevelt's death. He had guessed that people might want to build a memorial to him one day. In 1941, he called Supreme Court Justice Felix Frankfurter into his office to give him suggestions for his own memorial. "I want it plain, without any ornamentation, with the simple inscription, 'In Memory of . . . ,'" Roosevelt had said. He suggested a memorial as small as his desk and as simple as an ordinary gravestone. Justice Frankfurter carried out his friend's wishes and dedicated a desk-sized, marble memorial to Roosevelt outside the National Archives building in Washington, D.C.

Although this small memorial to Roosevelt already existed, Congress and the commission went ahead with its plans to honor him with a large, grand memorial near those of other presidents on the National Mall. In the spring of 1974, architect Lawrence Halprin was selected to design the new memorial. His design included four outdoor galleries, or rooms—one for each of President Roosevelt's terms in office. Halprin said that he wanted to "highlight both the experience of living through the FDR presidency and also the profound influence he had on our nation and on the world."

Before he could create his design, Halprin had to make some decisions. He wanted to build the

Sculptor Leonard Baskin (left) and architect Lawrence Halprin (right) work with the model for the third room of the memorial.

walls with a type of stone that Roosevelt would have liked. Roosevelt used reddish-gray fieldstones typically found in New England to build his library in Hyde Park, New York, and Val-kill, a retreat for Eleanor. Halprin could not find a similar, suitable stone in New England. In 1975, he found a rose-colored stone, called Carnelian granite, on the border between South Dakota and Minnesota. More than 6,000 tons of granite were used to build the 12-foot (3.7-meter) walls of the memorial.

Removed from the Cold Spring granite quarry, this stone was nicknamed "the mother stone." Before it was shaped, the stone measured 30 feet (9.14 m) long and 6 feet (1.83 m) high.

Once Halprin found the stone, he began choosing sculptors to create bronze statues for the memorial. Five American artists— Leonard Baskin, Neil Estern, Robert Graham, Tom Hardy, and George Segal—spent years working on their particular contributions to the memorial. Estern took ten years to complete his work: a statue of Roosevelt sitting with his loyal dog, Fala, and another of the president's wife, Eleanor. (This statue is the first one to honor a First Lady at a presidential memorial.) To get the details just right, Estern looked through hundreds of photographs. He visited the White House and other places where the president lived and worked. His research helped him decide which clothes and facial expression the statue might include.

Sculptor Neil Estern studies the leg (one of twenty-two pieces) of the FDR statue in 1996. Plaster casts of the scale models Estern used are on the left.

Estern and the other sculptors created nine sets of bronze sculptures in the memorial to tell the story of Roosevelt's leadership and the experience of many Americans during his presidency. Besides sculptors, Halprin needed other people to help him complete the memorial. Several people suggested quotations from Roosevelt's speeches that might be inscribed in the stone. A historian studied them and suggested words that would best express the president's achievement. Later, a stone carver cut the quotes into the granite. Landscape artists selected and planted the three hundred trees and three thousand shrubs that were added to the plantings already at the site.

Stone carver John Benson (left) at work on the FDR Memorial. Neil Estern (below, right) perfects the clay of FDR's Scottish Terrier, Fala. Made of two pieces, the statue was later cast in bronze.

One of the commission's guidelines was that the memorial should include water. Water was important to Roosevelt. Growing up near the Hudson River and vacationing on Campobello Island, he swam and sailed often. After his bout with polio, he exercised in water. In addition, some of his most important meetings as president were held on ships. So Halprin included waterfalls in his design to symbolize the significance of water to the president. The waterfalls would also help to mask the

FDR and British Prime Minister Winston Churchill met on board the USS Augusta *in August, 1941. Their meeting is known as the Atlantic Conference.*

sounds of planes taking off and landing at a nearby airport.

Before the construction work could begin, however, the 7.5-acre (3-hectare) site had to be strengthened. The soil around the Tidal Basin was too soft to support the weight of more than 31,000 stones. The walls would sink. In 1994, workers drove 900 steel pilings (or posts) down to solid ground 80 to 100 feet (24.4 to 30.5 m) below the surface. Then they covered the pilings with a concrete slab to support the weight of the memorial. The final cost of the memorial—including transporting the granite and sculpting the statues—was approximately $48 million.

During the first winter of its construction, the FDR memorial's steel-piling support system is visible above the snow.

On May 2, 1997, approximately seven thousand people attended the dedication ceremony of the Franklin Delano Roosevelt Memorial. President Bill Clinton, Vice President Al Gore, their wives, members of Congress, and some of Roosevelt's grandchildren were present. Some people, though, attended for another reason. They were upset that Estern's statue of Roosevelt did not show his wheelchair, cane, or leg braces. Some people believed that the memorial should acknowledge the president's disability, not hide it. Earlier in the week, Congress passed legislation recommended by President Clinton that would add a statue of Roosevelt in a wheelchair. Work on this sculpture is still to come, and the sculptor for the new statue has not been chosen. Although many

In July 1996, workers help to position blocks of granite in room four of the memorial.

16

are pleased with the project's approval, others think it is wrong to show the president in a wheelchair when the public never saw him in one. Despite the controversy, the Franklin Delano Roosevelt Memorial is the first in Washington, D.C., designed to be wheelchair-accessible. More than four million people visited the memorial in 1998.

As visitors enter the FDR Memorial, Roosevelt's name, title, and years in office appear on the first of many granite walls. The first room takes visitors back to his first term (1933–1937) as president. At his first inauguration on March 4, 1933, Roosevelt said, "The only thing we have to fear is fear itself." These bold, famous words are now carved into the granite wall. Below them, a bronze panel sculpted by Robert Graham shows Roosevelt waving to a crowd from an open car. The first of many waterfalls rumbles close by. Visitors also see an inscription of Roosevelt's promise to provide answers to the nation's problems: "I pledge you, I pledge myself, to a New Deal for the American people." At this point, the mood of the memorial is upbeat, almost bright. It reflects the hope that many people had as Roosevelt pushed a record number of new laws through Congress to ease the Depression during his first one hundred days in office.

In order to improve the economy, Roosevelt believed the government had to become more involved in people's lives. He asked Congress for government aid to farmers, protection for people's bank accounts, and assistance for struggling industries, such as oil. Congress voted for many of his programs. A popular Roosevelt program was the Civilian Conservation Corps (CCC). Founded in 1933 to help people find jobs, this program put 250,000 young, healthy men to work. Each worker was paid $30 a month and given a room and food at a CCC camp. By 1935, more than 500,000 "soil soldiers" (as they came to be known) were laying telephone lines and railroad

CCC workers in 1937

tracks, fighting fires, and planting trees.

In 1935, Roosevelt introduced the Social Security Act. It required working Americans to give up a small amount of their paychecks so that the money could be given to elderly people who could no longer work. In a sense, the program forced people to save money for their old age.

Even though Roosevelt worked hard to solve the country's problems, people still suffered. Many American workers had no regular source of income. Some people did not have enough money to buy food. They stood in lines at soup kitchens. Some searched through garbage in hopes of finding food. Environmental disasters in the Midwest and the Southwest added to the nation's woes. A terrible drought (lack of rain) and overfarming destroyed millions of acres of farmland. Many farm families headed to California in search of jobs as fruit and vegetable pickers, but the huge number of needy families proved overwhelming. There simply wasn't enough food, work, and housing to go around. President Roosevelt kept these problems in mind as he and his advisors tried to improve the nation's economy.

A breadline in New York City during the Depression

Two farm families from Purcell, Colorado, move their belongings in 1937 as they head west in search of jobs.

As visitors move into the memorial's second room, which marks Roosevelt's second term (1937–1941), the images become more disturbing. Americans felt confident enough in Roosevelt to reelect him, but the country was still torn by the Depression. These words from his second inaugural address on January 20, 1937, appear in the second room: "I see one-third of a nation ill-housed, ill-clad, ill-nourished." Sculptor George Segal captures the despair of those who lived on the farms and in the struggling cities with his bronze statues of an elderly farm couple and of five men in a breadline. The farm couple looks destitute and discouraged. Next to them are men from a city, standing in line waiting for food alongside a brick building. Their eyes are downcast, and the first man has his arms crossed as though he is anxious for the door to open. For them and so many like them, there seemed to be little hope.

Sculptor George Segal (above) works with an early model of the farm couple. In the final sculpture, the woman is sitting instead of standing. The sculpture of the farm couple (left). Unlike the statues of Franklin and Eleanor Roosevelt, the man and the woman in Segal's work are each made of one piece.

Roosevelt continued to work on the nation's problems. In one part of the second room, Segal's statue shows a man leaning toward an old-fashioned radio. (Television sets did not exist in the 1930s, but most families owned radios.) He listens intently to one of President Roosevelt's fireside chats that were broadcast on the radio. In these informal evening talks, the president explained his plans for solving the country's problems. He began his fireside chats with the comforting words, "My friends. . . ." The American public appreciated Roosevelt's kindness and willingness to communicate with them, and he was the first president to use the radio to talk directly to the American people.

"Fireside Chat," by George Segal. He wanted to portray how intently people listened to Roosevelt.

People listened as Roosevelt started discussing a new topic during the final two years of his second term—war in Europe. Germany's leader, Adolf Hitler, wanted to take over Europe. First, Germany seized Austria and Czechoslovakia. Then, in 1939, Germany invaded Poland. In response, France and Great Britain declared war on Germany, and World War II began.

Despite the bad news, many Americans were too concerned with their own struggle for survival to be troubled about a war across the Atlantic Ocean. They wanted to stay out of the war in Europe. But people grew more concerned when France surrendered to Germany, leaving the British to battle the Germans alone.

No president had ever been elected three times, but most Americans trusted Roosevelt's leadership. They wanted a president with experience in case the United States went to war. They voted him into office for a third term, which started in 1941.

This headline in the New York Times *announces Germany's invasion of Poland on September 1, 1939, the day World War II began in Europe.*

By that time, Great Britain's air force had been almost completely destroyed, and Germany was bombing Britain's cities relentlessly. In one of his most famous fireside chats, Roosevelt cleverly outlined a way to help Great Britain without involving American troops. "Suppose my neighbor's house catches fire," he said, "and I have a length of garden house 400 to 500 feet away. If he can take my garden hose, and

President Roosevelt during a fireside chat in April 1935

connect it to his hydrant, I may help to put out his fire. . . . If it goes through the fire all right, intact, without any damage to it, he gives it back to me . . . and if the hose was damaged by the fire, he could simply replace it." This story was his way of explaining to the American public how it could lend Britain (and other countries) military supplies that could be returned after the war. On March 11, 1941, Congress passed a law, the Lend-Lease Act, based on Roosevelt's plan.

By supplying war materials to fight Germany, the United States hoped to stay out of the war across the Atlantic. Unfortunately, more trouble began across the Pacific Ocean. Japan had joined forces with Germany and Italy. Like Germany, Japan wanted to take over other countries, such as China. When the U.S. government tried to stop Japan, the Japanese decided to go to war against the United States. On December 7, 1941, Japanese airplanes attacked a U.S. naval base in Pearl Harbor, Hawaii. In minutes, eight battleships were hit, along with many other cruisers and destroyers. At least 3,500 people lost their lives. It was the worst naval disaster in U.S. history. On December 8, the United States declared war on Japan. Three days later, on December 11, Germany and Italy declared war on the United States. Americans were officially involved in World War II.

Battleships during the attack on Pearl Harbor on December 7, 1941

When Lawrence Halprin was designing the third room of the memorial, he wanted visitors to sense the battles during Roosevelt's third term (1941–1945). In this room, large, rough chunks of granite symbolize the chaos of war. Here, the mood of the memorial becomes menacing. The waterfall in this room does not flow gently over a smooth wall. Instead, it thunders loudly down rocks scattered in harsh patterns. Roosevelt's declaration, "I have seen war . . . I hate war," is carved on the wall and also on some of the boulders.

The fountain and the "I have seen war. . ." inscription in the third room of the FDR Memorial

Although the third room of the memorial symbolizes war, it includes something peaceful—the 8' 7.5" (2.63-m) statue of Franklin Delano Roosevelt. Sitting beside it is the 35-inch (88.9-centimeter) statue of his Scottish terrier, Fala. After the chaotic stones and roaring falls, the larger-than-life statue of Roosevelt seems imposing and strong. He was the people's anchor. His statue is the calming centerpiece of the memorial.

The bronze statue of Franklin Delano Roosevelt weighs approximately 1,500 pounds (680 kilograms). In contrast, his dog, Fala, weighs approximately 225 pounds (102 kg).

Franklin Roosevelt never lived to see the end of World War II. He died in 1945, just three months into his fourth term. As visitors enter the fourth and final room of the memorial, they come to an overlook. It is a place to think about the past and the future. A ramp leads down to a pool that reflects Leonard Baskin's bronze mural of the funeral procession. It shows grieving people following Roosevelt's horse-drawn casket to the Capitol. This mural captures the sadness that swept the nation when President Roosevelt died. Nearby is a solitary statue of his widow, Eleanor, depicting her work for the United Nations after his death. A corner waterfall includes stepping stones, inviting visitors to feel the force and energy of the water, symbolizing these qualities in the

president. From this room, people can see the Washington Monument and the Thomas Jefferson Memorial. Roosevelt dedicated the Jefferson Memorial in 1943, and he was working on a speech to honor Jefferson when he died.

The Franklin Delano Roosevelt Memorial ends on a positive note. In four dramatic lines at the end of the fourth room, the granite walls trumpet the four key freedoms that President Roosevelt outlined in a speech on January 6, 1941:

Freedom of speech
Freedom of worship
Freedom from want
Freedom from fear

Although Americans were fighting for these freedoms during the Great Depression and World War II, most people have them today thanks to President Franklin Delano Roosevelt. His legacy lives on.

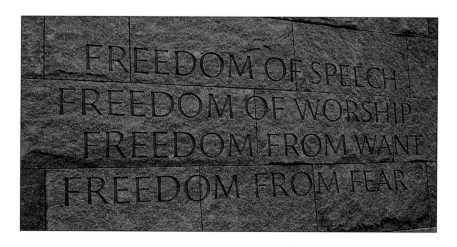

The "four freedoms" that Roosevelt spoke of are inscribed on the walls of the fourth room of the FDR Memorial.

GLOSSARY

architect – a person who designs buildings and oversees their construction

breadline – a line of people waiting to receive free food

breadline

bronze – a yellowish-brown metal that is a mixture of copper and tin and sometimes other elements; bronze is used for statues, bells, machine parts, and other things

chaos – great confusion or disorder

economy – the way in which the resources of a country, community, or business are managed

granite – a hard rock that is used in buildings and monuments

hemorrhage – heavy or uncontrollable bleeding

inauguration – a ceremony before a person takes an office

landmark – a familiar or easily seen object or building that marks or identifies a place

legacy – something transmitted by or received from a person from the past

memorial – something that is put up, kept, or done to help people continue to remember a person, group, or thing

mural – a work of art that is part of a wall or ceiling

National Mall – a rectangular park in the center of Washington, D.C., that is surrounded by museums, monuments, and government buildings

polio – a contagious disease caused by a virus that can cause paralysis by attacking the spinal cord

sculptor

sculptor – an artist who makes sculptures

symbolize – to stand for or represent something else

Tidal Basin – a pool dug along the Potomac River to help prevent flooding in Washington, D.C.

TIMELINE

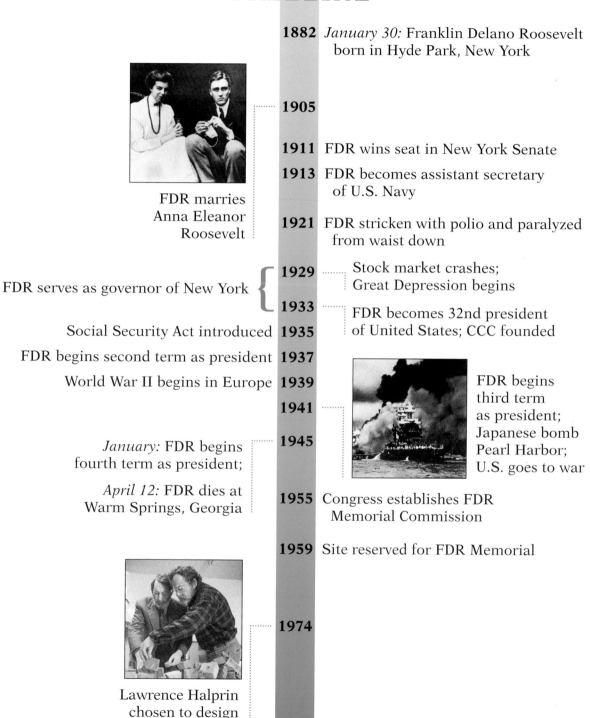

1882 *January 30:* Franklin Delano Roosevelt born in Hyde Park, New York

1905

FDR marries
Anna Eleanor
Roosevelt

1911 FDR wins seat in New York Senate

1913 FDR becomes assistant secretary of U.S. Navy

1921 FDR stricken with polio and paralyzed from waist down

FDR serves as governor of New York {

1929 Stock market crashes; Great Depression begins

1933 FDR becomes 32nd president of United States; CCC founded

Social Security Act introduced **1935**

FDR begins second term as president **1937**

World War II begins in Europe **1939**

1941 FDR begins third term as president; Japanese bomb Pearl Harbor; U.S. goes to war

January: FDR begins fourth term as president; **1945**

April 12: FDR dies at Warm Springs, Georgia

1955 Congress establishes FDR Memorial Commission

1959 Site reserved for FDR Memorial

1974

Lawrence Halprin chosen to design memorial

1997 *May 2:* Dedication of Franklin Delano Roosevelt Memorial

INDEX (*Boldface* page numbers indicate illustrations.)

PHOTO CREDITS

Photographs ©: AP/Wide World Photos: 2 (Brian K. Diggs), 7, 18, 20; Archive Photos: 14; Corbis-Bettmann: 5 top, 6, 31 top; Diane Smook: 12, 13 bottom, 30 bottom; Folio, Inc.: cover, 27 (Walter Bibikow); Lawrence Halprin: 13 top (John Benson), 15 (Dan Morris), 11, 16, 21 top, 31 bottom; Life Magazine © Time Inc.: 9 (Ed Clark); Mae Scanlan: 21 bottom, 28 right; Photri: 1, 22, 26, 28 left, 29 (Microstock); Stock Montage, Inc.: 23 (The New York Times), 8, 24; Superstock, Inc.: 5 bottom, 19, 25, 30 top, 31 center. Maps by TJS Design

PICTURE IDENTIFICATIONS

Cover: The statues of FDR and Fala are in the third room of the memorial.
Page 1: The bronze breadline statue by George Segal is in room two of the FDR Memorial.
Page 2: An aerial view of the Franklin Delano Roosevelt Memorial (right), the Tidal Basin (left), and the Thomas Jefferson Memorial (upper left)

ABOUT THE AUTHOR

Anne Phillips is a freelance writer and editor. She lives near Washington, D.C., and her research interests include twentieth-century history and American presidents.